Here and Now, There and Then

Here and Now, There and Then

Poems by

John Lawrence Darretta

© 2024 John Lawrence Darretta. All rights reserved.
This material may not be reproduced in any form, published,
reprinted, recorded, performed, broadcast,
rewritten, or redistributed without
the explicit permission of John Lawrence Darretta.
All such actions are strictly prohibited by law.

Cover design by Shay Culligan
Cover photo by Steven Grubiak

ISBN: 978-1-63980-555-6

Kelsay Books
502 South 1040 East, A-119
American Fork, Utah 84003
Kelsaybooks.com

For my mother and father

Acknowledgments

I am grateful to my dear family, friends, and students who read my poems throughout the years and offered their comments and suggestions that always made me rethink, revise and move on. I would like to thank Alexandra Paige and Steven Grubiak for their reading, correcting, and commenting on my manuscript.

Sincere acknowledgement is given to the publications and online venues in which the following poems (some in earlier versions) first appeared:

The Cape Cod Times: "Mourning Dove"

The Catholic Poetry Room: "A Whisper in the Wind," "Molten Glass"

The Cornelian: "The Voice of the Turtle"

The Inditer: "Petrus"

Nature's Wheel (Kelsay Books): "Nature's Wheel"

The Pilgrim Journal: "Heaven's Hoard"

YouTube: "Lady of Life," "The Manger"

Many thanks to Karen Kelsay, Jenna Wray, and the staff at Kelsay Books for their pleasant assistance throughout the editing and publication of *Here and Now, There and Then*.

Contents

Prologue

Litany of Life   15

I. Here and Now: The Physical World of Time

The Sower	19
An Exodus	20
The Sincerity of Siloam	21
Invocations	22
Petrus	23
Modern Magdalene	24
The Sky Is Red	25
A Bird in the Rafters	26
Lady of Life	27
The Manger	28
Night Song	29
Easter Springs	30
Nature's Wheel	31
My First Spelling Lesson	32
A Tango of Temptation	33

II. There and Then: The Spiritual World of Eternity

A Child's Plea	37
Divine Nature	38
A Whisper in the Wind	39
Molten Glass	40
Gentle Breeze of Spirit	41
Heaven's Hoard	42
The Voice of the Turtle	43
Mourning Dove	44
Heaven's Harvest	45

The Saving Cross	46
What Happens?	47
Helix	48
As I Enter the Chapel of Myself	49
Faith	50
All Things	51

Epilogue

I Am Always With You	55

Prologue

Litany of Life

*I never know God until I am held so close to him
that there is nothing in between.*
—Julian of Norwich

                    beginning and ending
                and that which is in between

here and there
and that which is in between

now and then
and that which is in between

day and night
and that which is in between

dark and light
and that which is in between

cold and hot
and that which is in between

wet and dry
and that which is in between

rough and smooth
and that which is in between

good and bad
and that which is in between

young and old
and that which is in between

black and white
and that which is in between

weak and strong
and that which is in between

wise and foolish
and that which is in between

pain and pleasure
and that which is in between

birth and death
and that which is in between

                         God and I
                  and nothing in between

I.

Here and Now:
The Physical World of Time

The Sower

Ambling like autumn leaves
drifting like clouds of spring
departing like mountain streams
that rush to feed the lowlands.

Leaves, we go alone, we come together
clouds, we drift apart, we join each other
streams, we leave one place and find another.

Why dispersion yet adhesion?

Where we go, we take ourselves
and a share of all we love,
we scatter like seeds that fly
in wind but fall to new ground.

An Exodus

When I met you on the desert's edge
we left our lyres on the willow

we lost our sorrowful tears
in the waters of Babylon
then we smiled at Cana's feast

we watched them dancing on the wall
going to and fro, to and fro

now playing our mended harps
we will go, we will go

singing and dancing down all His streets

The Sincerity of Siloam

*Blessed are your eyes, because they see,
and your ears, because they hear.*
                              Matthew 13:16

by the waters of Siloam
people are opening their mouths
their words falling out like spittle

spittle drops to hard ground
not mixing with earth to make mud
that opens an eye or heals an ear

by the waters of Siloam
people are opening their mouths
their words falling out like spittle

I cannot see opening mouths
I cannot hear the falling spittle

by the waters of Siloam
I wait for One who is to come

Invocations

Like a cyclic rosary
designed for a universe
of different milieu
$E=mc^2$ in beads
humming mantras
tied in Hebraic knots
woven on a prayer mat
with evangelic chords
breathless from turning
too many prayer wheels.

We are strung together
linked to one another
each a pearl
touching lives
spirit breathing
curved and bowing
between all the decades
with divine devotion
in the womb of the world
toward a circle of eternity.

Petrus

They said he was a liar
        and could not walk
            the water of his tears.

But he emptied
        nets full of grace
        because cocks kept crowing
        in his ears.

He had to learn to fish,
        to fill and feed.

He had to learn to live,
        to love and lead.

But, first,
        pride had to smash
        against the rock.

He had to learn to be still.
        and climb from the drifting boat
        onto the water of his tears.

Modern Magdalene

Stark vermillion falling
to naked feet.

Sharp cinnamon lingering
sadly sweet.

Once gone astray
then the right way.

Love and invoked by hand-filled faces
in a cathedral's empty aisles.

Scoffed and mocked by earthly cheapness
with purple-pink parasols in Place Pigalles.

The Sky Is Red

    Matthew 16:1–4

The golden summer days
have soft-melted away.

The feeling of warmth
has slow-driven on.

Autumn's colors
of orange-brown
have folded up
and left the town.

As winter hardens,
within the middle
of a darken gray Saturday
I wonder what will Sunday bring?

A Bird in the Rafters

I long for a bird in the rafters,
The crow of a rooster or two
And heed the dove's moans of hereafters
For them and for me and for you.

I long for a lamb at the cradle,
The rustling of wings in the hay
And resist long shadows that laden
The sky and the hills on the way.

I long for a king at the manger,
A shepherd who pipes a sweet song
To lessen the discord of danger
And the gloom of waiting so long.

I long for a holy child again,
A maiden who lightens with birth
Sparking the flying flames of amen
For peace and good will on God's earth.

Lady of Life

Morning light of Nazareth, on the Galilee,
the air rebounds with angel sounds,
and Mary turns to hear.

Holy star of Bethlehem, searching far and wide,
wise men look for a mighty king,
and Mary shows her child.

Trembling glow of Golgotha, at the sacred cross,
where Jesus' love moves death to life,
and Mary gives her heart.

Lady of life who broke the night,
who birthed the son and brought us light,
bring us to God's love.

The Manger

I saw the manger of a child
With figures red and gold.
Among hay and incense
A silver bell that tolled,
Of wise men sent by distant kings,
Of shepherds under angels' wings,
Whose garments flung in full motion
For all the world to know

A star that filled the universe
With incandescent glow,
A son to fill the universe
With inexpectant love.

I saw the manger of a child
With white birds in the eaves.
Calves of brown on the ground
And lambs lay in the leaves,
As Joseph watched with careful eye
And Mary scanned the darkened sky,
The cradled Jesus lifted
A simple hand to show

A star that filled the universe
With incandescent glow,
A Son to fill the universe
With inexpectant love.

Night Song

All is calm
all is starlight and hay.

All lamb bleating
and ox breathing
bending warm wind
and biting frost.

All faith seeking
and hope sharing
shining rich find
and saving host.

All is starlight and hay
all is calm.

Easter Springs

Watch the Easter of a whitening
In the gilded blood of the rising
In the purple tomb

What tomb?
That Tomb

Where the golden crocus beats
To the time of thunder
And the rose rain flowers

Where the April womb
Breeds for everyone

Nature's Wheel

When Nature's Wheel revolves my day in light and shadow
moves wind and rain among the seasons
letting the budding life of spring with stem to leaf and flower
quiver to summer's bounty at the height of the sun
then fall into autumn's amber and fade toward wintry white,
I wait for the wheel to turn again.

When Nature's Wheel surrounds my life in growth and languor
shifts the depth of grief to crest of joy
making the silence or the noise with its failure or success
waver what appears today into gone tomorrow
from the robe of childhood's call toward the pall of pending death,
I wait for the wheel to turn again.

My First Spelling Lesson

In the beginning was the WORD,
and the word was GOD,
and it was GOOD.
He made all things,
and they were GOOD.

When we learn
that everything
GOD made is GOOD,
and the second
"O" is OURSELVES

We find GOD in all things.

A Tango of Temptation

Just when I think I'm St. Francis
in the serpent prances,
up from the well
with fetid smell
of ruin and tarnation.

As soon as Satan advances
in the Spirit dances,
that dove from above
with fragrance of love
for me and all creation.

The skip of the snake and the dove,
a tangle of hate and love,
the music gets louder,
the steps even faster,
spinning to a grand farewell.

Promenade, swing, of pas de deux,
a graceful movement or two,
and with stumbling times seven,
do I turn to blissful heaven,
or twist to a blistering hell?

II.

There and Then:
The Spiritual World of Eternity

A Child's Plea

I've known this world before
no ampler place to live.
A child at Eden's door
with hands held to forgive.

Now I see blur below
and nothing clear above.
The world in want and fear
so empty without love.

Come, O Lord, come again
and let all evil cease.
Come, O Lord, come again
to set the world at peace.

Divine Nature

We grow and mature
within time and space
through our early youth,
into adulthood, and to death
the union of body and soul,
physical and spiritual

so to be born again to wit
the union of soul and spirit
child of holiness
in all peacefulness
for eternity and infinity
to live and abide with divinity.

A Whisper in the Wind

Word
whirled in the wonder of creation
wrought in the wood of the sacred cross
whispered in the wind of Pentecost

Word
filling my mouth
and expanding my heart
inform and unfold me
bending, pierce me
with pointedness
and let me speak
letters of Love

Molten Glass

Soft colors slowly shift along the ancient chancel wall,
trails of light beaming through a tinted window at my back,
as from without, above the whir of traffic and stir of life,
burning sun pierces the glass, suffusing inherent hues,
streaming them on the wall like a magic lantern of divinity.

Under a shade of stillness, I watch the projected prism,
floating from red to orange, yellow, green, blue to violet,
then it turns to wax and wane, slow crawl and rest,
brushing over and through my eyes with a palette of pigments,
saffroned, azured, and crimsoned with dyes of warm light.

It is the yellow-orange glare that invites and envelops,
and I do not know if it is my affinity for marigold or tangerine,
smoldering sunlight or trembling flick of candle flame,
but it draws like a fragrance of God suddenly palpable,
as if turning a corner of the garden into a rush of lilac.

All too soon, the sun's rays lift me over the nebulous blush,
where I am gathered into molten glass, coaxed on a color wheel
to a place I know, bright and boundless, where I blend
with the blazing light and when, for a shining moment,
I lose all heavy darkness.

Gentle Breeze of Spirit

A three-armed fan revolves on the church ceiling,
where the light from below creates a shadowed version
that whirls and crosses from center to left and right,
a triune ghost fan revolving around the real fan,
a playful image of the one.

Air streams down the cloistered walls,
drifts across the fading floor, enfolds the faithful
who respire to the turning trio that sends it high again,
a gentle breeze of spirit, breathing in and out, down and up,
the three in one gathering all in one.

The light of faith affirms the shadow selves
as they unfold along the ceiling to embrace all below.
In the light, one cannot separate shadow from substance.
How complete the fans; how well they turn to heal
and comfort in the heat of day.

A flutter of perception flows from fan and shadows,
where there is the one and the manifestations of the one.
The fan shadows are not the fan, but could not exist without it.
Separately they are three; together they are one.
It is the breath of light that makes it so.

Heaven's Hoard

High in a corner of the church's stone roof
sun has leaked through stained glass
weaving shafts of golden gleams and silvered streaks,
brushing curves with tufts of blue, splashing emerald and rose,
where remains of cries and prayers are cradled in tinted shadows
under a light of heaven and hope.

Nestled in the arch are faithful echoes of pleas and praise
for ease from illness, end of loneness, cease from fear,
of gratitude for wedding bliss, thanksgiving for a job,
glee for a newborn, from worry of ageing, sorrow of death,
and with all pledges of renewal, pangs of doubt,
appeals for forgiveness, and calls for peace.

High in a corner of the church's stone roof
trembling treasures of emotion, some as ancient as the stones,
float at the vaulted edge, mixing with chanted tones,
organ bells and strain of harps, lifting with linger of incense,
bouquet of lily and snuff of candlewick, here and there,
of past and present, old and new.

Time and space hold no sway in the sacred canopy of the church,
where all is hallowed hoard, reflections of confession and prayer,
impressions of hope and despair, hidden in the soft folds of light,
sparkling jewels of dust that have risen beyond the roof
to endless peace and boundless love, encased in a sacred place
and enshrined in a corner of the heart.

The Voice of the Turtle

Wind has kissed the trees,
the dark rains are gone,
and beneath bitter earth
expectant life trembles
to a touch of warmth.

A chanting bird prostrates
on top of a stone wall,
as flitting golden bees
sip on the honeyed words
from light lips of clover.

On rays of blazing sun,
chrism scents slow linger
from obedient grains
attending to strong command
to free the captured balm.

Like raindrops on the sea
the word is on the tongue,
a phrase of holy wheat,
crushed in shady darkness,
caressed in binding light.

Believing hands espoused pointing
heavenward like stalwart cedars
tipped with New Jerusalem's gold,
while wailing feet of wending souls
are crossing on dry barren plains
to climb the flowering hills.

Mourning Dove

A gray mourning dove
perched on a bowed branch
sits alone with memories
and scans the leaden sky
looking for what is no longer here
as if someone could appear from a cloud.

Cooing and moaning sighs
are songs of the lonely dove
sad chants while waiting on the limb
with cries of long lament
listening for its lost mate
as if a voice would call from a wind.

No more the shared branch
or double dive to the garden
to pick and peck together
now feeding alone in the grass
fetching for what is no longer there
as if a body should bud from a bush.

Somber solo flying with whisper wings
not the darting duo from the bough
no more turns in cool air to catch the glow
while from the shade it coos and cries
for a burning blast of hopeful sun
as if love might alight from a fire.

My gray mourning dove
bells are tolling in the distance
the sky is clear and the air is calm
come this way—reach for me—
and through the flood of our affection
bring me a branch from the bow in the clouds.

Heaven's Harvest

Bring us to the garden,
to gather grape and wheat.
Lead us to the table,
to worship and to eat.

Feed our need, Lord Jesus,
provide us from above.
Soothe our thirst, Lord Jesus,
fulfill us with your love.

Share Your bread and wine, Lord,
gather us together.
Give Your blood and body,
grant us life forever.
Through Mary, blood and body;
from Jesus, bread and wine.
Through Mary, Son of God;
from Jesus, Love Divine.

The Saving Cross

How still the air on distant hills,
    How still the howling valley breeze.

How calm the rivers and the streams,
    How calm the wide and troubled seas.

How still the vineyards and the groves,
    How still the tossed and battered sheaves.

How calm the shepherds and the sheep,
    How calm the birds in trembling trees.

It's Golgotha I see
    with fires at a loss,

        And still and calm
        is Jesus on the Saving Cross.

        And still and calm,
        is Jesus on the Saving Cross.

What Happens?

When the thrust of life is to prolong
    rather than to live
And death is just an end
    rather than a means
When creation owes more to science
    and less to art
And love
    is more lust and no trust
When music
    makes noise not melody
And learning
    is indoctrination not education
When truth
    belongs to a thinking subject not an object of thought
And happiness
    is possessing things not a rush of joy
When evil
    is good
And Good
    is evil?

Things
 f
  a
   l   l   a   a   t   p   r . . .

Helix

A base spiraling upward
each hour of the day spiraling upward
each day of the year spiraling upward
each year of a life spiraling upward

each life spiraling upward
never horizontal
but always vertical
a helix spiraling upward

choices made on the way
bumps in the twisting road

As I Enter the Chapel of Myself

who are all these
that I can feel
sitting here next to me?

what are all these
splattered shadows
of grand mortality?

where are they from
all different
in such variety?

when do they come
so quietly
in such expectancy?

why do they all
appear to me
vivid and lovingly?

and He answered,
"They are another Myself."

Faith

It's that time again,
and leaves on trees
are dusty brown,
once so beautiful
blue flowers are bent
and bruised dark purple,
while glaring through
bare tawny twigs,
a frail burning bush
grieves for green grass
that's now long gone,
as changing earth
pales and hardens.

Patiently,
they all wait
to brightly bloom again.

All Things

All things have
beginning and end
with a middle in between
whether woman or man
        flower or lamb

All things have
height and weight
with a depth in between
whether tiny or tall
        portly or small

All things have
time and place
with a story in between
whether year or minute
        town or planet

All things have
darkness and light
with a shade in between
whether pain or play
        nighttime or day

All things have
start and finish
with a trail in between
whether race or game
        failure or fame

All things reveal
the three in all—
that trinity of reality.

Epilogue

I Am Always With You

I am always with you
      I am the Father
           I am the Son
                  I am the Holy Spirit

I am always with you
      In Birth
           In Life
                  In Death

I am always with you
      Here and There
           Near and Far
                  In Heaven and On Earth

I am always with you
      Past and Present
           Then and Now
                  Tomorrow and Today

I am always with you
      In Happiness and in Sorrow
            In Pleasure and in Pain
                  In Faith and in Doubt

Come with Me
      Be with Me
           Stay with Me
                  I am always with You

About the Author

A former metropolitan New York college professor, John Lawrence Darretta now lives on Cape Cod. John holds a Ph.D. in English from Fordham University and has authored books and articles on American literature and Italian cinema. As Fulbright Professor to Italy, he taught at universities in Milan and Turin, where he studied Italian film at Museo Nazionale del Cinema. A specialist on Italian films of the neorealist period, his *Vittorio De Sica,* published by G. K. Hall, was the first full-length work in English on the films of the noted director. He is also author of *Before the Sun Has Set: Retribution in the Fiction of Flannery O'Connor (*Peter Lang Publishing). He recently authored *Sacred Senses in Sacred Space: A Journey into a Church* (Gatekeeper Press).

For John, writing poetry has been a passion since high school days. His creative work has appeared in *America Magazine, Penwood Review, Avalon Literary Review, Pilgrim Journal, Haiku Journal, First Literary Review-East,* and other venues. A collection of his poems has been published in *Nature's Wheel* by Kelsay Books